My First Pocket Guide

CALIFORNIA

By Carole Marsh

The California Experience

Correlates with the CCS California Content Standards

The GALLOPADE GANG

Carole Marsh
Bob Longmeyer
Michele Yother
Michael Marsh
Sherry Moss
Chad Beard
Sue Gentzke
Cecil Anderson
Steven Saint-Laurent
Deborah Sims
Andrew Brim
Andrea Detro
John Raines
Karin Petersen
Billie Walburn
Doug Boston
Kim Holst
Jennifer McGann
Ellen Miller
William Nesbitt, Jr.
Kathy Zimmer
Wanda Coats

Published by
GALLOPADE INTERNATIONAL

www.thecaliforniaexperience.com
800-536-2GET • www.gallopade.com

Character Illustrations by Lucyna A. M. Green.

Other California Experience Products

- The California Experience!
- The BIG California Reproducible Activity Book
- The Coolest California Coloring Book
- My First Book About California!
- California "Jography": A Fun Run Through Our State
- California Jeopardy!: Answers and Questions About Our State
- The California Experience! Sticker Pack
- The California Experience! Poster/Map
- Discover California CD-ROM
- California "Geo" Bingo Game
- California "Histo" Bingo Game

A Word From the Author... (okay, a few words)...

Hi!

Here's your own handy pocket guide about the great state of California! It really will fit in a pocket–I tested it. And it really will be useful when you want to know a fact you forgot, to bone up for a test, or when your teacher says, "I wonder . . ." and you have the answer–instantly! Wow, I'm impressed!

Get smart, have fun!

Carole Marsh

California Basics explores your state's symbols and their special meanings!

California Geography digs up the what's where in your state!

California History is like traveling through time to some of your state's great moments!

California People introduces you to famous personalities and your next-door neighbors!

California Places shows you where you might enjoy your next family vacation!

California Nature - no preservatives here, just what Mother Nature gave to California!

All the real fun stuff that we just HAD to save for its own section!

Who Named You?

California's official state name is...

State Name

California

Word Definition

OFFICIAL: appointed, authorized, or approved by a government or organization

Statehood: September 9, 1850

California was the ***31***st state to join the Union.

What A Great Name!

California is named for a mythical paradise, *Califia*, from a Spanish romance written by Montalvo in 1510. Explorer Juan Cabrillo and his men knew the story of the island and the gold and jewels, but the Spanish actually found very little gold.

What's In A Name?

California is not the only name by which the state is recognized. Like many other states, California has several nicknames, official or unofficial!

The El Dorado State

Grape State

GOLDEN STATE

The Land of Milk and Honey

State Capital:
Sacramento

Many people came to this area after gold was discovered. By 1849, it was named Sacramento because it was near the Sacramento River. In 1854, Sacramento became the final state capital.

John Sutter named his land grant *Nueva Helvitia*, which means new Switzerland.

The state capital was moved from San Jose to Monterey, Vallejo, Benicia, and San Francisco between 1850 and 1854.

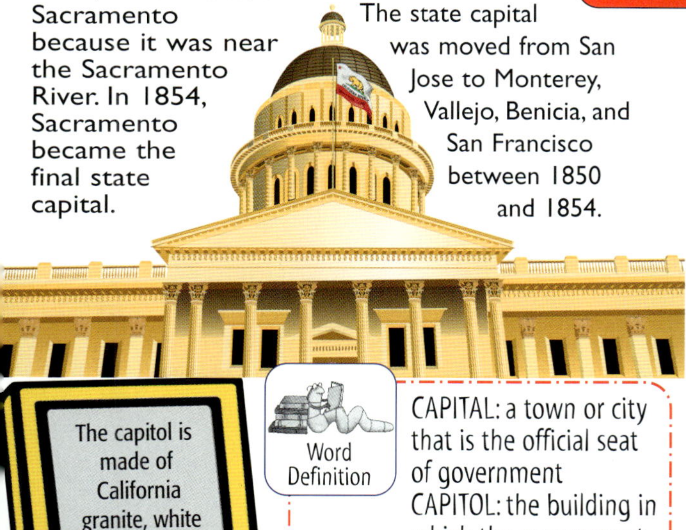

The capitol is made of California granite, white painted brick, and topped by a huge gold dome.

Word Definition

CAPITAL: a town or city that is the official seat of government
CAPITOL: the building in which the government officials meet

Sacramento was the terminus, or ending point, of the famous Pony Express Route across the west.

Who's in Charge Here?

California's GOVERNMENT has three branches:

LEGISLATIVE

California citizens can vote to elect their chosen representatives.

Two Houses: the Senate (40 members); Assembly (80 members)

EXECUTIVE

A governor, lieutenant governor, and other constitutional officers

JUDICIAL

Supreme Court a chief justice plus six other justices

If someone wants to change California's constitution, a proposition must first be made by the legislature, voter initiative, or constitutional convention. Then people vote on the issue during an election. It will only become law if a majority of the voters approve the proposition.

State Flag

California's Flag has a red star in the upper left-hand corner. The California grizzly bear represents the many bears once seen in the state. "California Republic" and a red band are beneath the star and bear. A group of men who called themselves *Osos*, Spanish for bears, were part of the Bear Flag Revolt of June 14, 1846, at Sonoma.

State Seal

Adopted in 1849, California's seal has a grizzly bear, Minerva, the Roman goddess of wisdom, and a miner.

Word Definition

MOTTO: a sentence, phrase, or word expressing the spirits or purpose of an organization or group

State Motto

Eureka

Eureka is a Greek word which means, "I have found it!" Miners found a lot of gold in California.

Adopted in 1849, the motto refers to the discovery of gold in the Sierra Nevada.

Birds of A Feather

The state bird of California is the California Valley Quail.

The California Valley Quail has distinctive head feathers.

State Tree

California Redwood

Sometimes the California Redwood grows by itself, and sometimes, it grows in groves alongside a variety of other cedar and pine trees such as the Douglas fir and the canoe cedar.

Golden Poppy

At the request of the Society of Colonial Dames in California, the Golden Poppy became California's state flower in 1901.

The Golden Poppy grows wild all over the state. Sometimes the flowers are called flame throwers.

State Animal

California Grizzly Bear

Settlers hunted the California grizzly bear because of the threat to people and livestock. There are no more wild grizzlies left in California. The last wild grizzly bear in California died in 1922.

RIDDLE: If the state flower got mixed up with the grizzly bear, what would you have?

ANSWER: A golden grizzly... or a poppy bear?

Serpentine

Serpentine is California's state rock. It's used to make asbestos and contains the minerals chromite, magnesite, and cinnabar.

Benitoite (Blue Diamond)

California's state gem is Benitoite, or the blue diamond. It was first discovered in the San Benito River. It ranges in color from pale blue to dark sapphire blue.

California was the first state to choose an official state rock in 1965.

Saber-toothed Cat

California's state fossil is the saber-toothed cat. Many specimens of the saber-toothed cat were preserved in Los Angeles' La Brea tar pits.

Gold

California's state mineral is gold. California is called the Golden State.

California Desert Tortoise

State Reptile

The California desert tortoise can live longer than humans. The tortoises are protected by law.

It is illegal to move a desert tortoise from its native habitat... but you can move them off the road!

State Song

I Love You, California

Words by F.B. Silverwood, music by A.F. Frankenstein

I love you, California, you're the greatest state of all;
I love you in the winter, summer, spring, and fall;
I love your fertile valleys; your dear mountains I adore;
I love your grand old ocean, and I love her rugged shore.

Where the snow-crowned Golden Sierras
Keep their watch o'er the valleys' bloom;
It is there I would be, in our land by the sea,
Ev'ry breeze bearing rich perfume,
It is here nature gives of her rarest.
It is Home Sweet Home to me,
And I know when I die, I shall breathe my last sigh
For my sunny California.

I love your redwood forests–love your fields of yellow grain;
I love your summer breezes, and I love your winter rain;
I love you, land of flowers; land of honey, fruit, and wine;
I love you California; you have won this heart of mine.

I love your old gray missions-love your vineyards stretching far;
I love you California, with your Golden Gate ajar;
I love your purple sunsets, love your skies of azure blue;
I love you, California; I just can't help loving you.

I love you, California, you are very dear to me;
I love you, Tamalpais, and I love Yosemite;
I love you, land of sunshine, half your beauties are untold;
I loved you in my childhood, and I'll love you when I'm old.

California Gray Whale

The California Gray Whale migrates up and down the California coast. They spend the winters in the warm waters of Baja California and the summers in Alaska's Bering Sea. There are no more gray whales left in the Atlantic Ocean. Most of the gray whales in the Pacific Ocean can be found in the Eastern Pacific along the California Coast.

California Dog-Face Butterfly

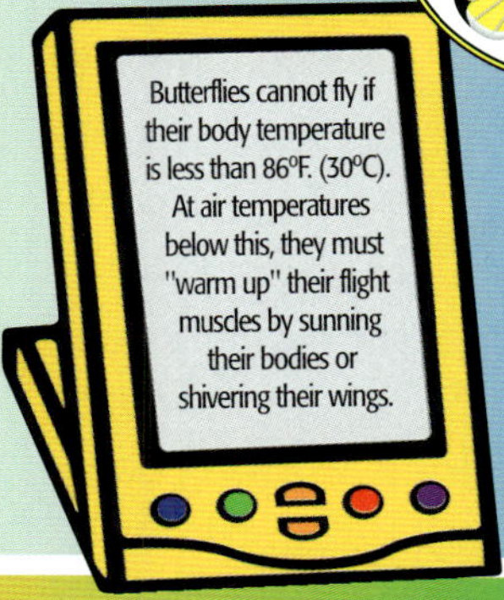

In 1929, entomologists voted to pick the state insect, and the dog-face butterfly won. You will recognize it from the two spots on its wings. The spots look like the eyes of a dog.

Golden Trout

The Golden Trout is native to the high Sierras of California. It is found only in high elevations in very clear and deep bodies of water. It has been successfully transplanted in other places but only near its origin.

Golden Trout are golden on the bottom with a long pink and red stripe on the sides. The top of the fish has black spots.

Tasty Trout

Put a trout filet on foil. Drizzle with lemon juice. Sprinkle with salt and pepper. Add shredded smoked ham and broil fish until done.

California Map

California's shape is formed mostly by the Pacific coast on the west and the Sierra Nevada ranges in the east.

California's northern border cuts directly through the Klamath and Cascade Mountains.

California Map

State Location

California is on the western shore of the United States. The state forms much of the United States' western border.

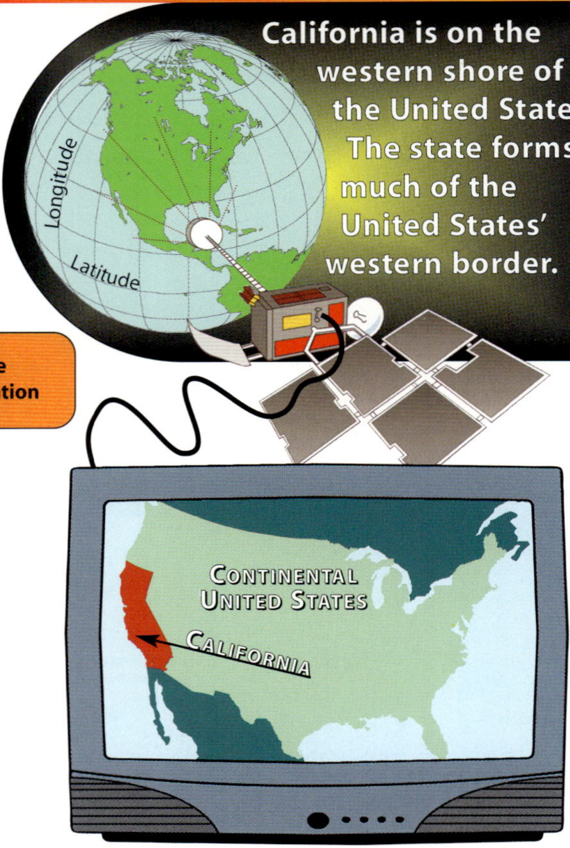

Word Definition

LATITUDE: Imaginary lines which run horizontally east and west around the globe
LONGITUDE: Imaginary lines which run vertically north and south around the globe.

On The Border!

These border California:

States: Oregon, Nevada, Arizona

Body of water: Pacific Ocean

Country: Mexico

You Take the High Road!

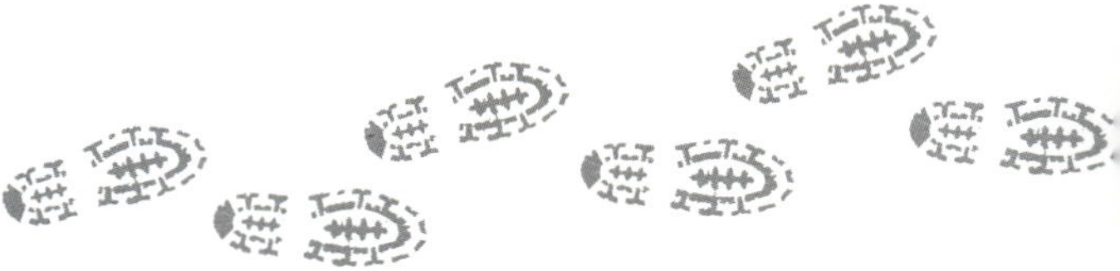

California is 250 miles (402 kilometers) east to west... or west to east. Either way, it's a long drive!

Total Area: Approx. 158,869 square miles
Land Area: Approx. 155,973 square miles

California is 770 miles (1,239 kilometers) north to south... or south to north. Either way, it's a REALLY long drive!

And I'll Take the Low Road!

Highest & Lowest Points

HIGHEST POINT

Mount Whitney—14,494 feet above sea level (4,418 meters)

Mount Whitney in Inyo-Tulare County is California's highest point, and the highest point in the contiguous United States.

LOWEST POINT

Bad Water in Death Valley at 282 feet (85.9 meters) below sea level

Death Valley is the hottest and driest place in the U.S. with temperatures reaching 115°F (46°C). California's highest and lowest points are within 100 miles (161 kilometers) of each other.

I'm Countying on You!

California is divided into 58 counties

Word Definition

COUNTY: an administrative subdivision of a state or territory

San Bernadino County has about three million acres (1,215,000 hectares) and is the largest county in the U.S.

Natural Resources

Forests make up about 45% of California's land area

Word Definition

NATURAL RESOURCES: things that exist in or are formed by nature

Minerals:

- Oil
- Natural gas
- Sodium sulfate
- Boron
- Gypsum
- Magnesium
- Pumice
- Tungsten

Deep-water ports allow large ships to deliver and export goods around the world.

Weather, Or Not?!

California's climate depends on which part of California you're in. Because California is such a large state, the weather on any day could be very different in a different part of the state.

Highest Temperature: 134°F (57°C) at Death Valley on July 10, 1913

°F=Degrees Fahrenheit °C=Degrees Celsi

Lowest Temperature: -45°F (-43°C) at Boca on January 20, 1937

BACK ON TOP

California's topography includes four land areas:

COASTAL MOUNTAIN RANGES

SIERRA NEVADA

CENTRAL VALLEY

THE GREAT BASIN

California is a land of tall mountains, low valleys, dry deserts, rich farmlands, and coastal islands.

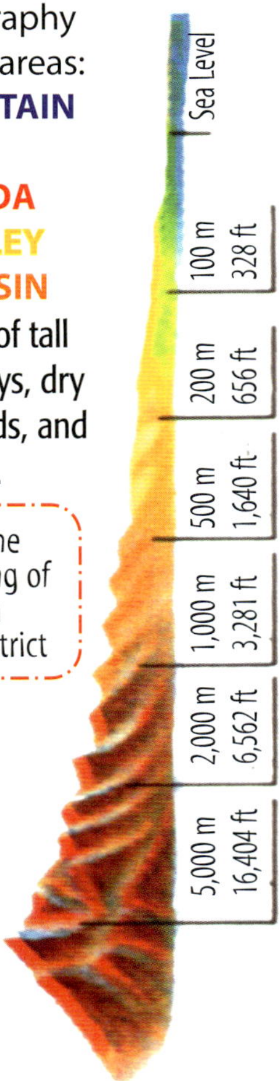

Word Definition

TOPOGRAPHY: the detailed mapping of the features of a small area or district

The San Andreas Fault has created California's mountains, and every time you feel the earth shake, they may be getting bigger!

King of the Hill

Here are some of California's major mountains and ranges.

Mountains

Mount Whitney
Lassen Peak
Mount Shasta
Mount Baldy
Mammoth Mountain

Ranges

Sierra Nevada
Sierra Madre
Tehachapi Mountains
Cascade Range
Klamath Mountains
Coastal Ranges

The profile of the Tamalpais Mountain looks like a sleeping Native American girl.

Down the River

Snow in the Sierra Nevadas melts in the spring and fills California riverbeds.

Here are some of California's major rivers.

Major Rivers

- American
- Sacramento
- San Joaquin
- Colorado
- Pit
- Feather
- Merced
- Mojave
- Owens
- Tuolumne

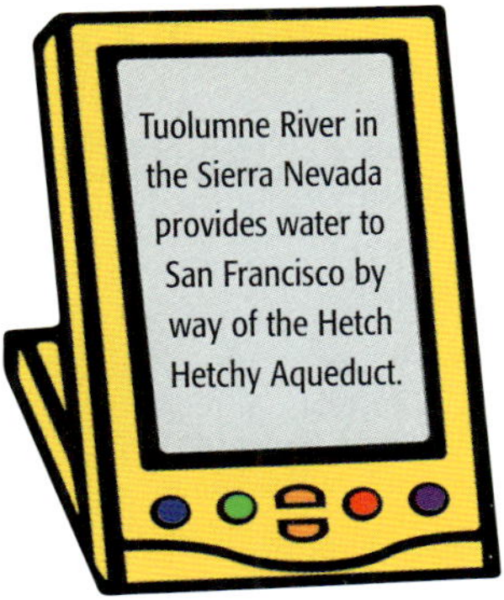

Gone Fishin'

Major Bodies of Water

Early farmers diverted the Colorado River from its original course into the Imperial Valley. It was controlled for several years before it overran its banks and flowed for two years into Salton Sink. Today the Salton Sea is one of the largest lakes in California.

- Lake Tahoe
- Goose Lake
- Mono Lake
- Salton Sea
- Shasta Lake
- Clear Lake
- Monterey Bay
- Folsom Lake
- Lake Berryessa
- Eagle Lake
- Sacramento Delta
- San Francisco Bay
- Lake Oroville

Word Definition

SINK: a low-lying, poorly drained area where water collects.

Mono Lake is one of the world's oldest lakes at 700,000 years o

HOME TOWNS

Have you heard these wonderful California city, town, and crossroad names? Perhaps you can start your own

LARGER TOWNS:

Los Angeles
San Diego
San Jose
San Francisco
Long Beach
Fresno
Anaheim
San Bernadino
Sacramento
Oakland
Riverside
Santa Ana
Stockton
Santa Barbara

SMALLER TOWNS:

Bodfish
Chico
Diamond Springs
Raisin
Red Bluff
Smartville
Desert Center
Quartz Hill
Inverness
Grizzly Flats

Transportation

Major Interstate Highways

I-5, I-8, I-10, I-15, I-40, I-80

The Santa Fe Trail, Oregon Trail, and California Trail were important early "highways."

Railroads

Transpor-tation

The Transcontinental Railroad played a role in California's early history. Today California has about 6,530 miles (10,509 kilometers) of railroad track.

Major Airports

Los Angeles
San Francisco
San Diego

Seaports

Los Angeles
Oakland
San Diego
Long Beach
San Francisco Bay

Timeline

1542	Juan Rodríguez Cabrillo explores San Diego Bay
1769	Junípero Serra establishes first mission at San Diego
1822	California becomes part of Mexico
1846	U.S. settlers protest Mexican rule in Bear Flag Revolt
1848	Mexico surrenders California to U.S.;
	Gold discovered at Sutter's Mill
1849	Gold Rush begins; First state constitution written
1869	Transcontinental railroad connects California to East
1906	San Francisco devastated by earthquake and fire
1930	Dust Bowl immigration from Midwest
1936	Hoover Dam provides power and water
1937	Golden Gate Bridge opens
1965	Racial riots in Watts
1960s	Computer industry transforms Silicon Valley
1989	Major earthquake strikes San Francisco area
2001	California enters 21st century

Here come the humans!

As early as 9500 B.C., Paleo (ancient) people lived in California. They may have originally come across a frozen bridge of land between Asia and today's Alaska. If so, they slowly traveled south until some settled in what would one day become the state of California. Native Americans used black volcanic glass, found in the mountains of Mono County, to make arrow points.

Native Americans Once Ruled!

Native Americans lived in California before the first Europeans arrived. The Native Americans practiced complex religions, hunted small animals with flint arrowheads, and gathered acorns and other vegetation. Coastal Native Americans also caught fish and shellfish to eat. At the time of the first European explorers, the major tribes in California were the Na-Den, Hokan, Penutian, and Aztec-Tanoan.

Word Definition

WAMPUM: beads, pierced and strung used by Indians as money, or for ornaments or ceremonies.

Land Ho

In the early 1600s, California was shown on maps as an island, and it was thought correct for about 100 years. Early explorers searched for a mythical channel called the Strait of Anian. They hoped that this channel would link the Atlantic and Pacific Oceans.

Home, Sweet, Home

Spanish navigator Juan Cabrillo first sighted California in 1542. In 1579, Sir Francis Drake claimed the coast of Northern California for England. Later, Russian fur traders traveled up and down the coast of California, but it was almost another 200 years before any Europeans settled the area!

Governor Gaspar de Portolá of Baja California Mexico set up the first presidio near San Diego in 1769. Franciscan friar Junípero Serra, the Gray Ox, established the first mission that same year. By 1823, the Franciscans had built 21 missions in all stretching from San Diego to north of San Francisco Bay. In addition to the first presidio, the Spanish built others and created small farming communities known as pueblos.

Russian fur traders built Rossiya (Fort Ross) in 1812 north of San Francisco. In 1839, the Russians were ordered by the Czar to abandon their colony.

"Thar's Gold in Them Thar Hills!"

Native Gold is California's state mineral. John Sutter started a farm and a lumber mill. One of his workers, James Marshall, discovered gold in the American River. By 1849, the California Gold Rush was on! People came from all over to search for gold. These people were called prospectors. If they decided to stay and dig for gold, they were called miners. Later they were called '49ers. Sutter's Fort grew with the gold rush and later became the capital city, Sacramento.

California remains one of the top gold-producing states. Gold worth $15-20 million is mined every year.

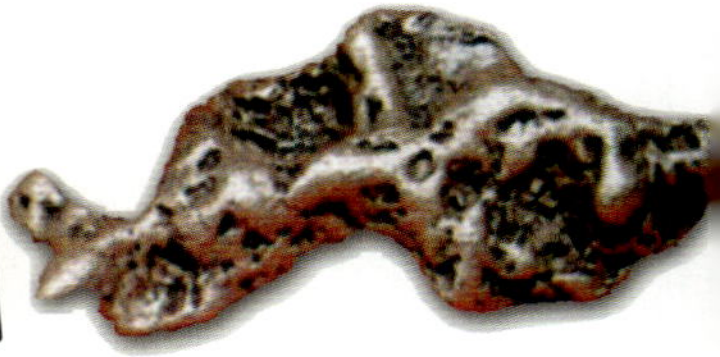

Look 'em Up!

Find out more about these California legends!

- Walter "Death Valley Scotty" Scott, was a shameless self-promoter who reached legendary status.

- Emperor Norton I, English born self-proclaimed Emperor of the United States and Protector of Mexico, and subject of San Francisco legend.

- Devils Hole in Death Valley is home to a Piute legend. A city called Shin–au–av is said to lie beneath the valley in a forgotten cave.

Of Human Bondage

Americans most often associate African-Americans with slavery. However, the early Franciscan friars and Spanish soldiers captured Native Americans and settled them into a life of servitude.

Native Americans near California's coast were forced to work as farm laborers and built the mission buildings under the direction of Franciscan missionaries. Under Mexican rule, slavery in California was abolished in 1829.

In 1849, California's first state constitution was approved by popular vote and prohibited slavery. The issue of slavery and states' rights led to the Civil War. The 13th amendment to the U.S. constitution ended slavery in America and all areas under its jurisdiction.

Bear Flag Revolt!

During the Bear Flag Revolt of June 14, 1846, a group of American settlers revolted against Mexican rule.

Raising the Bear Flag in Sonoma, settlers declared California an independent republic. The republic did not last very long though. On July 7, 1846 Commander John C. Sloat of the U.S. Navy claimed California for the United States.

Brother

The Civil War was fought between the American states. The argument was over the right of the states to make their own decisions, including whether or not to own slaves. Some of the southern states began to secede (leave) the Union. They formed the Confederate States of America. The fighting occurred mostly in the eastern U.S., but the Californio Andres Pico formed a battalion that distinguished itself in the Civil War.

Word Definition

RECONSTRUCTION: the recovery and rebuilding period following the Civil War.

vs. Brother

The *Shenandoah*, a Confederate warship, sailed along the California coast in 1865 seeking out Union trade ships or whaling vessels. Union troops were stationed on Catalina Island during the Civil War.

The Civil War

Federal troops captured a Confederate group, the Showalter Party, southeast of Los Angeles in 1861.

Get It In Writing!

Declaration of Independence, 1776, written by Thomas Jefferson

U.S. Constitution, 1787, The Constitution went into effect in 1789.

Treaty of Guadalupe Hidalgo, 1848

California's first state constitution, 1849

California's present constitution, 1879

Famous Documents

WELCOME TO AMERICA!

Californians have come to the state from other states and many other countries on almost every continent! As time has gone by, California's population has grown more diverse. This means that people of different races and different cultures and ethnic backgrounds have moved to California.

The Gold Rush was the first major event to bring many immigrants to California. People from the United States, Mexico, and many other countries began migrating to California. By 1852 there were as many as 20,000 Chinese living in San Francisco. Beginning in 1910, immigrants to San Francisco were processed at Angel Island in San Francisco Bay. The Dust Bowl immigration from the Midwest began about 1930. Although these people were largely Americans, the culture in areas reflected the changes. Bakersfield is called the "Okie Capital" of California for the many people who came from Oklahoma.

1906

Earthquake and fire devastates San Francisco

1965

Race riots cause much destruction in Watts

1969

Mud-slides kill 100 and damage 10,000 homes

1991

Fires destroy homes in Oakland-Berkeley area

1994

Earthquake shakes Los Angeles

Legal Stuff

1882

Exclusion Act banned Chinese Immigration

1933

Repeal of Prohibition; important to California wineries

1965

Immigration and Nationality Act

1994

O.J. Simpson murder trial rivets nation

1996

Proposition 209 repeals affirmative action

Women

1910

Alice Wells of L.A. becomes the nation's first policewoman.

1920

Women gain suffrage nationally through the 19th Amendment.

1923

Mae Ella Hunt Nolan elected California's first congresswoman.

1974

March Fong Eu elected first Asian-American woman to state-wide office as Secretary of State.

1982

Gloria Molina becomes the first Hispanic woman elected to the state assembly.

1992

California elects two women senators: Barbara Boxer and Dianne Feinstein.

Word Definition

SUFFRAGE: the right or privilege of voting

Fight!, Fight!, Fight!

Wars that Californians participated in:

- **Mexican Revolution**
- **Mexican-American War**
- **Civil War**
- **Modoc War**
- **Spanish-American War**
- **World War I**
- **World War II**
- **Korean War**
- **Vietnam War**
- **Persian Gulf War**

Manzanar National Historic Site memorializes the unfortunate imprisonment beginning in 1942 of Japanese Americans during World War II.

Hooray for Hollywood!

Los Angeles was the location of the very first motion picture theater, which opened April 2, 1902. Later, Hollywood got a head-start over Europe in the film industry because of World War I. In 1927, the first movie with sound, *The Jazz Singer*, was released and changed entertainment forever. Now the Academy of Motion Picture Arts and Sciences presents the "Oscars" every year to the best and brightest in the film industry.

Indian Tribes

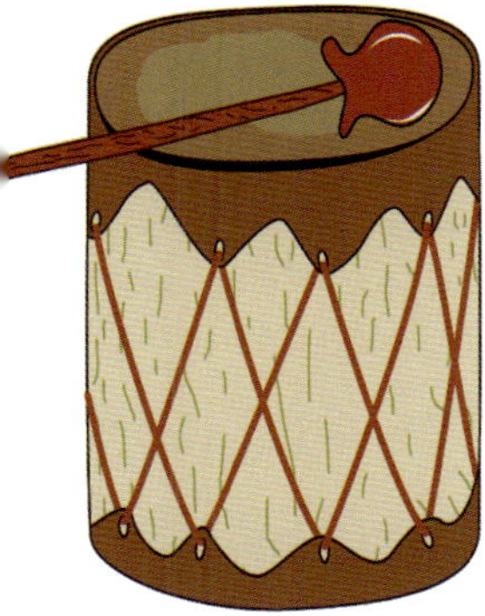

- Hoopa
- Paiute
- Yurok
- Karok
- Modoc
- Yahi
- Cherokee

California has 96 Federal Indian Reservations. Most of these areas are small. Native Americans often live in small communities called *rancherias*.

In 1969, a Native American group called "Indians of All Tribes" claimed Alcatraz Island for themselves and some remained there until they were removed by U.S. troops in 1971.

A man called Ishi was the last surviving member of the Yahi tribe. This sole survivor was discovered in 1911. He was very scared and there was no one left who spoke his language.

Here, There, Everywhere!

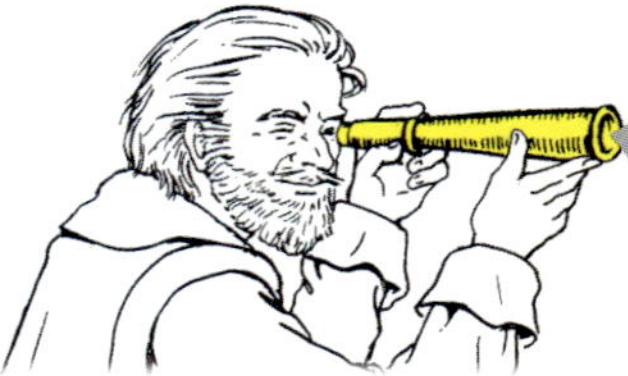

JUAN CABRILLO—first European explorer to reach California

FRANCIS DRAKE—explored the coast and claimed California for England

JUAN CRESPI—Spanish missionary and explorer

JUNÍPERO SERRA and GASPAR DE PORTOLÁ—founded California's first mission

JEDEDIAH SMITH—first American to reach California by land

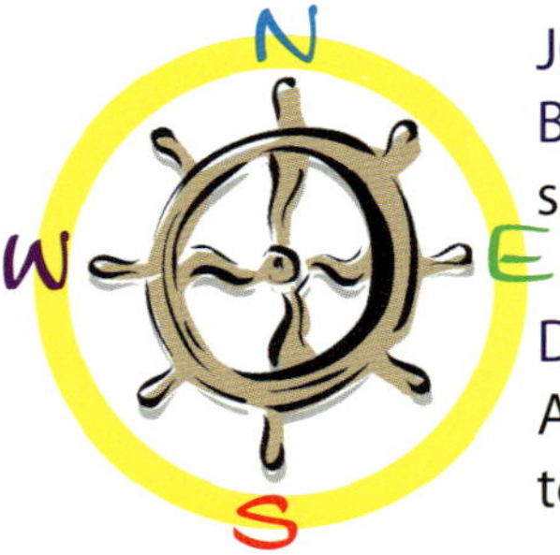

JOHN BIDWELL and JOHN BARTLESON—led first U.S. settlers to California!

DR. SALLY K. RIDE—first American female astronaut to explore space!

Founding Fathers

These Californians played especially important roles in the creation of the state!

SEBASTÍAN VIZCAÍNO—urged Spain to colonize California

JOHN AUGUSTUS SUTTER—settled present day Sacramento

ROBERT SEMPLE—leader of the Bear Flag Revolt, president of California's Constitutional Convention

JOHN C. FRÉMONT—led first U.S. government expeditions into California

MARIANO GUADALUPE VALLEJO—pioneer, commander, and member of the first state senate

Founding Mothers

BIDDY MASON—freed slave woman, prosperous Los Angeles philanthropist

JESSIE BENTON FRÉMONT—fought claim jumpers, and wrote many stories of her adventures

TOBY RIDDLE—Modoc Indian, married a U.S. settler, tried to keep peace between Native Americans and settlers

PHOEBE APPERSON HEARST—left millions of dollars to her son, William Randolph Hearst, when she died. Her son built the largest publishing empire the world had ever seen and even ran for president!

Heir to the Winchester Rifle fortune, Sarah Winchester believed that as long as construction continued on her house (Winchester Mystery House), she would not be harmed by spirits. When she died, her house had 160 rooms!

MIFFLIN GIBBS—first African–American judge in U.S.

WILLIAM LEIDESDORFF—first African–American diplomat in U.S.

TOM BRADLEY—first African-American mayor of Los Angeles.

MARY E. PLEASANTS—successful African-American business woman who challenged the railroad for not letting her ride the train in 1866.

ROBERT C. MAYNARD—first African-American to own a major newspaper, the *Oakland Tribune*.

Bandits

• Joaquin Murieta, a California outlaw, sought revenge on men who harmed his family.

• An Australian group of robbers called the Sydney Ducks was daring enough to rob San Francisco businesses during business hours!

• Charles Bolton, or Charles Boles (Black Bart), robbed stagecoaches using an empty shotgun, walked to and from the crime scene, and left short poems behind.

• Crime in San Francisco during the 1850s prompted Sam Brannan to create the Vigilante Committee.

• In early California, if a mine was left abandoned, claim jumpers would start working the mine, claiming the stake for themselves.

Criminals were held in a Federal Prison on Alcatraz Island. Al Capone and Machine Gun Kelley both served time at "The Rock." Because the prison was about a mile offshore, escape was unlikely.

Sports Figures

TIGER WOODS—Golfer

JOE DIMAGGIO—Baseball player

MARK MCGWIRE—Baseball Player

RICHARD (PANCHO) GONZALES—Tennis player

CHERYL MILLER—Basketball player

VENUS AND SERENA WILLIAMS—Tennis playing sisters; Grand Slam champions

Sports Figures

JAMES "GENTLEMAN JIM" CORBETT—World heavyweight boxing champion

MAX "MADCAP MAXIE" BAER—World heavyweight boxing champion

BILLIE JEAN KING—won record number of international tennis titles

Entertainers

★ ROBERT REDFORD—actor

★ DEXTER GORDON—musician

★ WARDELL GRAY—musician

★ CHARLIE CHAPLIN—pioneer silent film actor and director

★ CLINT EASTWOOD—actor, director

★ LOUIS B. MEYER—producer

★ MARILYN MONROE—actress

★ D.W. GRIFFITH—pioneer director and producer

★ CECIL B. DE MILLE—pioneer motion picture producer and director

★ JOHN WAYNE—actor

★ WALT DISNEY—pioneer motion-picture animator, producer

★ JERRY GARCIA—Grateful Dead musician

★ MERLE HAGGARD—Okie from Muskogee

★ BEACH BOYS—musicians

★ RITCHIE VALENS—musician

Sam Goldwyn, a Russian immigrant, became one of the founders of Hollywood.

PENS ARE MIGHTIER THAN SWORDS!

- JOHN STEINBECK—writer
- JACK LONDON—writer
- GERTRUDE ATHERTON—author
- DAVID BELASCO—playwright
- ROBERT FROST—Pulitzer Prize winning poet
- SYDNEY HOWARD—playwright
- WILLIAM SAROYAN—author
- ROBINSON JEFFERS—narrative poet
- UPTON BEALL SINCLAIR—Pulitzer Prize winning author
- JACK KEROUAC—author
- LINCOLN STEFFENS—journalist, author
- WILLIAM RANDOLPH HEARST—publisher
- FRANCIS BRETT HARTE—writer, publisher
- PAUL CONRAD—Pulitzer Prize winning cartoonist
- CZESLAW MILOSZ—Nobel Prize winning author
- WILLIAM SAROYAN—Pulitzer Prize winning writer
- EUGENE O'NEILL—Nobel Prize winning playwright

John Steinbeck won the 1939 Pulitzer Prize for "The Grapes of Wrath," and the 1962 Nobel Prize in Literature.

nom de plume: French for pen name, a fictitious name a writer chooses to write under instead of his or her real name.

Sam Brannan, publisher of the *California Star*, is credited with starting the gold rush.

Artists

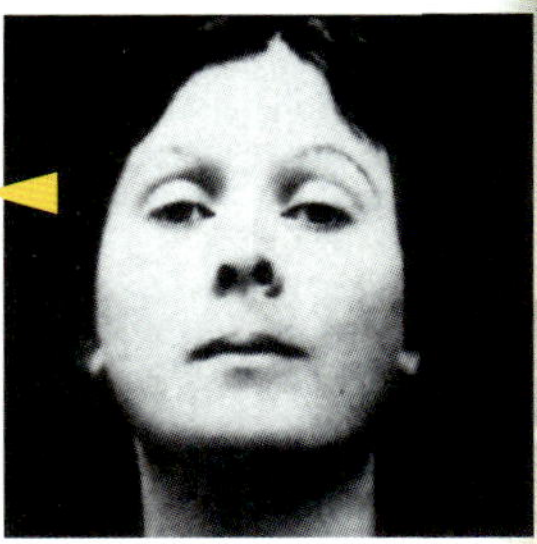

ISADORA DUNCAN—created interpretive dancing

DOROTHEA LANGE—photographer

ISAMU NOGUCHI—sculptor

ANSEL ADAMS—Photographer, Conservationist

Doctors and Scientists

LUTHER BURBANK—horticulturist

GEORGE ELLERY HALE—astronomer

JOSEPH LE CONTE—geologist

ÁGOSTON HARASZTHY DE MOKCSA—viticulturist

FAE MARGARET ADAMS—first woman doctor to receive a regular commission in the United States Army in 1953

JONAS SALK—developed first polio vaccine

ANDREW HALLIDIE—developed the San Francisco cable car system

Military Figures

MAJOR GENERAL JOHN C. FRÉMONT

COMMODORE ROBERT STOCKTON

AIR FORCE GENERAL JAMES H. DOOLITTLE

ULYSSES S. GRANT was stationed in California early in his career. From 1852-1854, Grant served at California's Fort Humboldt.

GENERAL GEORGE S. PATTON JR.

EDWARDS AIR FORCE BASE in the Mojave Desert was home to the first flight to break the sound barrier in 1947. CHUCK YEAGER was the first man to fly faster than Mach 1.

JEANA YEAGER and DICK RUTAN were the first pilots to fly around the world nonstop in the experimental plane, the *Voyager*. They took off and landed at EDWARDS AIR FORCE BASE.

The western headquarters for the U.S. CAMEL CORPS was once located near the summit of Tejon Pass!

Prize Winners

- Willard Libby—1960 Nobel Prize, chemistry, developed radioactive dating procedure
- Linus Pauling—1954 Nobel Prize, chemistry; 1962 Nobel Peace Prize
- Luis Walter Alvarez—1966 Nobel Prize, physics
- Owen Chamberlain—1959 Nobel Prize, physics
- Ernest Orlando Lawrence—1939 Nobel Prize, physics; 1957 Enrico Fermi Award
- Edwin Mattison McMillan—1952 Nobel Prize, chemistry; 1963 Atoms for Peace Award
- Glenn Theodore Seaborg—1951 Nobel Prize, chemistry; 1959 Enrico Fermi Award
- Maria Goeppert-Mayer—1963 Nobel Prize, physics
- Emilio Segre—1959 Nobel Prize, physics

Leaders

- Hiram Johnson—California governor, U.S. senator, leader of the Progressive Movement
- Richard Milhous Nixon—37th president
- Ronald Wilson Reagan—40th president
- Kintpuash (Captain Jack)—Modoc tribal chief
- John Muir—naturalist, crusader for the national park system, founder of the Sierra Club in 1892
- Cesar Estrada Chavez—organized United Farm Workers of America

- Ng Poon Chew—Chinese publisher-activist

About 8,000 pounds of jellybeans were included in the $8 million celebration of Ronald Reagan's inauguration!

- Anthony M. Kennedy—U.S. Supreme Court justice
- Annette Abbott Adams—first woman to hold office as U.S. assistant attorney general, first woman to be U.S. district attorney, and first woman to be assistant U.S. attorney
- Earl Warren—chief justice of the U.S. Supreme Court, wrote 1954 ruling outlawing racial segregation in public schools
- George Deukmejian—member of California assembly, state senate, state attorney general, and governor

Keeping the Faith

There are many missions, mosques, synagogues, churches and temples throughout California. A temple built with chapels for Taoism, Buddhism, and Confucianism was built at Oroville in 1863. The first Buddhist temple in the United States was constructed in San Francisco in 1905, and San Francisco is the headquarters of the Buddhist Churches of America. By the mid-20th century, Los Angeles was home to more Jews than anywhere in the world outside of New York and Israel.

SCHOOLS

Some of California's famous schools:

- California State Polytechnic University
- University of California at Berkeley
- University of California at Los Angeles
- California Institute of Technology
- Chapman University
- University of Southern California
- University of the Pacific
- Santa Clara University
- University of San Francisco
- Pepperdine University
- Point Loma Nazarene University
- Fresno Pacific University
- Stanford University
- La Sierra University
- Whittier College

California's first tax-supported public school opened in San Francisco in 1850.

Historic Sites and Parks

Historic Sites

- ★ Fort Point National Historic Site
- ★ San Francisco Maritime National Historic Park
- ★ Historic Fort Ross built by Russian fur traders in 1812
- ★ Monterey's Path of History
- ★ Andres Pico Adobe
- ★ Sutter's Fort State Historic Park

California's National Parks

- ★ Yosemite National Park
- ★ Sequoia National Park
- ★ Redwood National Park
- ★ Joshua Tree National Park
- ★ Kings Canyon National Park
- ★ Death Valley National Park
- ★ Lassen Volcanic National Park
- ★ Channel Islands National Park

Nine of the world's highest waterfalls are in Yosemite National Park.

California has more than 125 different state parks. The largest of these is the Anza-Borrego Desert State Park, which covers 600,000 acres (243,000 hectares).

Early Residency

★ John Muir National Historic Site—preserved mansion where the naturalist lived

★ Scotty's Castle—at Death Valley, home of legendary Walter E. "Death Valley Scotty" Scott

★ Hearst San Simeon State Historical Monument—residence of publisher William Randolph Hearst

★ Former home of author Zane Grey on Catalina Island. The pueblo style building overlooks Avalon Bay and has been converted into a hotel.

★ Bodie State Historic Park is maintained by the State Government as a Ghost Town! It looks a lot like it did as an 1849 boomtown.

A few of California's famous

Battles & Forts

- Fort Ross
- Fort Sutter
- Battle of the Old Woman's Gun–1846
- Bear Flag Revolt–1846
- Battle of San Pasqual–1848
- Fort Humboldt

- Fort Tejon
- Fort Mason
- Massacre on Indian Island–1860
- Fort Bragg
- Fort Point
- Fort Bidwell

Libraries

- **The Richard Nixon Library**, Yorba Linda

- **Ronald Reagan Presidential Library and Museum**, Simi Valley
- **Hoover Institution Library and Archives**, Stanford University

- **Bancroft Library**, University of California at Berkeley

- **Library of the California Historical Society**, San Francisco

- **California State Library**, Sacramento

Universal Studios, Hollywood

Monterey Bay Aquarium, Scenes for the movie *Star Trek IV* were filmed here.

Disneyland, Anaheim

Sea World, San Diego

Knott's Berry Farm, Buena Park

Fisherman's Wharf, San Francisco

San Diego Zoo, World famous San Diego Zoo has about 4,000 animals. There are Mongolian horses, Indonesian Komodo dragons, New Zealand kiwis, Australian koalas, and giant pandas.

Museums

- California State Railroad Museum
- Golden State Museum
- Crocker Art Museum
- Santa Barbara Museum of Art
- Oakland Museum of California
- J. Paul Getty Art Museum
- M. H. De Young Memorial Museum
- San Francisco Museum of Modern Art
- Los Angeles County Museum of Art
- Norton Simon Museum
- Natural History Museum
- Griffith Observatory and Planetarium
- California Museum of Science and Industry
- San Joaquin Pioneer Museum
- Norton Simon Museum

NATIONAL MONUMENTS

LAVA BEDS

DEATH VALLEY

DEVIL'S POSTPILE

JOSHUA TREE

PINNACLES

CABRILLO

MUIR WOODS

The San Francisco cable cars have been designated a national landmark!

SPACE PLACE!

Edwards Air Force Base is the largest aerospace research and flight-test facility in the U.S. The base is one of the landing sites for the space shuttle. It also has the longest runway in the world, which is about seven miles (11 km) long!

The Arts

ACADEMY OF MOTION PICTURE
ARTS AND SCIENCES

SAN FRANCISCO BALLET

LOS ANGELES PHILHARMONIC ORCHESTRA

OLD GLOBE THEATRE—San Diego

SAN FRANCISCO OPERA ASSOCIATION

BACH FESTIVAL—Carmel

FESTIVAL OF ARTS—Laguna

BUFFALO NIGHTS THEATER COMPANY

HEARST GREEK THEATER—University of California at Berkeley

SAN FRANCISCO SYMPHONY ORCHESTRA

Seashores & Lighthouses

Point Reyes National Seashore is California's national seashore.

California's coastline, from Oregon to Mexico, is 840 miles (1,352 kilometers) long.

Alcatraz became the home of the West Coast's first lighthouse in 1854. Now California has about 40 lighthouses!

THE PASADENA FREEWAY was America's first freeway, built in 1940. HIGHWAY 1, stretches 600 miles (966 kilometers) up the Big Sur Coast.

GOLDEN GATE BRIDGE spans the Golden Gate over San Francisco Bay, and connects San Francisco with Marin County.

OAKLAND BAY BRIDGE connects San Francisco with Oakland.

RAILROADS More passengers ride trains in California than in any other state except New York.

Caves and Caverns

California has more than 200 caves within Lava Beds National Monument located near Lassen Volcanic National Park. The caves were formed by melted rock rushing up through the earth.

Volcano

Lava Flow

Lava Bed

A *spelunker* is a person who goes exploring caves!

QUESTION:

- Which is the stalagmite?
- Which is the stalactite?

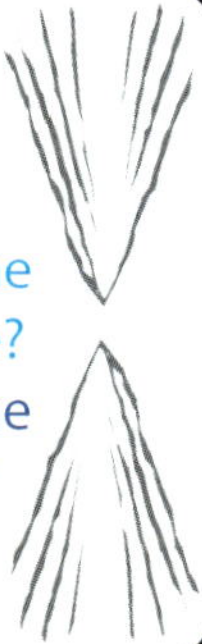

ANSWER: Stalactites are long, tapering formations hanging from the roof of a cavern, produced by continuous watery deposits containing certain minerals. The mineral-rich water dripping from stalactites often forms conical stalagmites on the floor below.

Animals of California

California animals include:

Mule Deer
Black Bear
Bobcat
Beaver
Raccoon

Cougar
Horned toad
Marmot
Fox
Weasel
Chipmunk
Rabbit
Gila monster

California Endangered Species

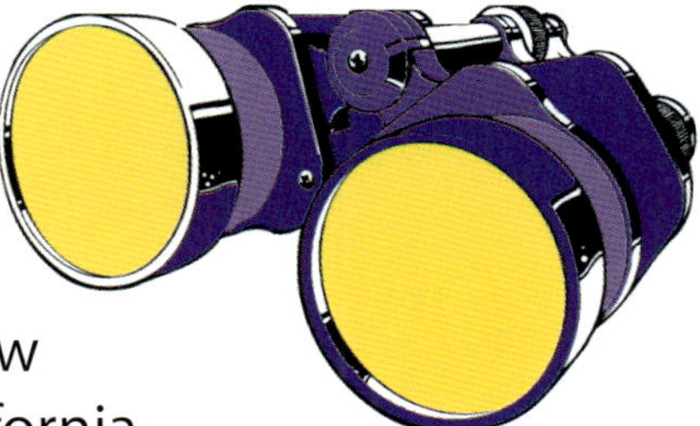

The mountains behind Santa Barbara are home to the few remaining California condors, the largest land bird in North America. They are an endangered species. This means that they are nearly extinct. Other endangered species include the riparian brush rabbit, and the fringe-toed lizard.

You may spy these birds!

Wood Duck

Steller's jay
Black-headed grosbeak
Western bluebird
Western tanager
Acorn woodpecker
Warbler
Bald eagle
Gull
Swallow
Pelican
Roadrunner
Murre

Quail

Wren

Mourning Dove

Tern

Thrush

A hummingbird's wings beat 75 times a second—so fast that you only see a blur! They make short, squeaky sounds, but do not sing.

Around March 19 every year, a flock of swallows returns to the mission at San Juan Capistrano.

Don't let these California bugs bug you!

Mayfly
Dragonfly
Damselfly
Field cricket
Stick insect
Termite
Giant water bug
Water strider
Spittlebug
Ant lion
Firefly
Weevil
Beetle

Bumblebee

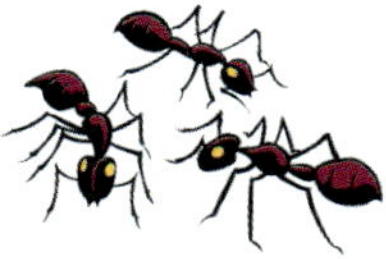
Ants

Butterfly

Praying Mantis

Ladybug

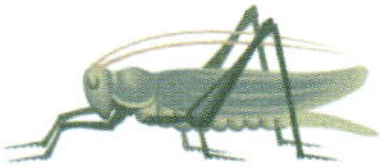
Grasshopper

Fish

Swimming in California waters:

Bass
Bluegill
Bream
Carp
Catfish
Crappie
Croaker
Flounder
Hogfish
Menhaden
Perch
Salmon
Steelhead
Sunfish
Trout

California is the only place in the world you'll find grunion.

Sea Critters

In California's seas, you may find:

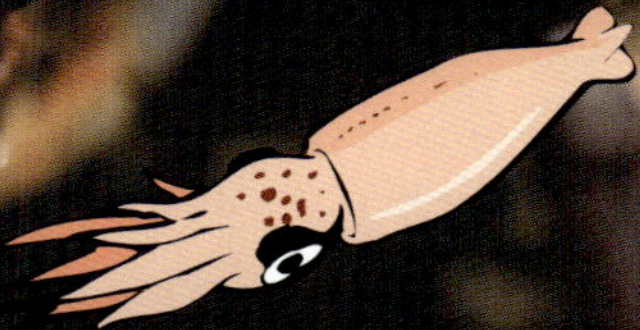

- Shark
- Crab
- Oyster
- Dolphin
- Grunion
- Porpoise
- Turtle
- Squid
- Whale
- Manta Ray
- Jellyfish
- Scallop
- Clam
- Skate

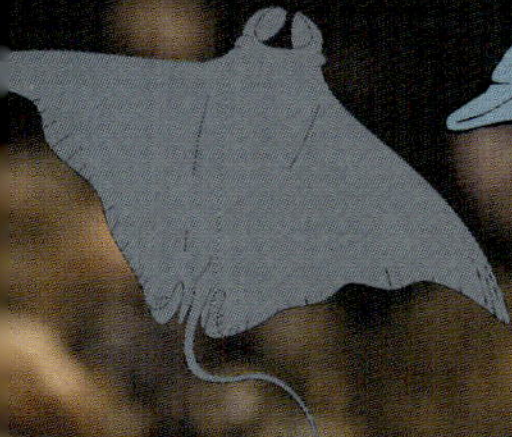

Bottlenose dolphins send messages to each other by whistling and squealing. They will help an injured dolphin get to the surface so it can breathe!

Seashells

She sells seashells by the California seashore.

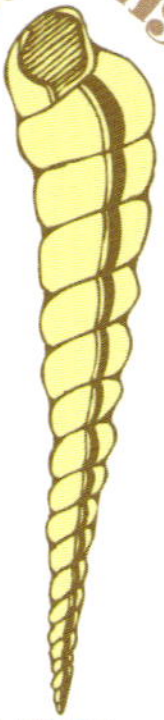
Auger Shell

- Chiton
- Limpet
- Abalone
- Top shell
- Cerith
- Slipper shell
- Worm shell
- Cowrie
- Bubble shell
- Wentletrap
- Whelk
- Murex
- Cone shell
- Vampire shell
- Tusk shell
- Mussel
- Cockle

Olive Shell

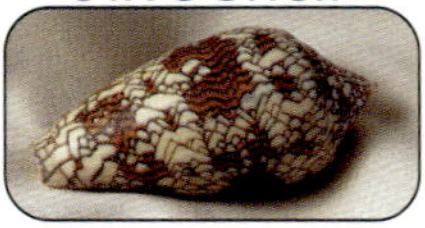

Periwinkle

Moon Shell

Abalones live beneath the high tide line on rocks. They live along North America's Pacific Coast.

Coquina

TREEMENDOUS!

THESE TREES TOWER OVER CALIFORNIA:

Bristlecone pine
Desert ironwood
California bay tree
Tanoak madrone
Ponderosa pine
Oregon maple
Redwood
Sequoia
Desert willow
Joshua tree
Sagebrush
Spruce
Juniper
Mesquite

The oldest living tree resides in the Prairie Creek Redwoods State Park near Orick. It's a 12,000-year-old redwood named "Eternal God." It measures 238 feet (73m) tall and 19 feet 7 inches (6 meters) in diameter!

Wildflowers

Are you crazy about these California wildflowers?

Violets
Columbine
Jacob's ladder
Spring beauty
Black eyed susan
Indian paintbrush
Buttercup
Butter-and-eggs
Goldenrod
Chicory
Fireweed
Oxeye daisy
Lupine
Globemallow
Prickly pear
Mariposa lily

A red trillium smells like rotten meat! This attracts flies, which pollinate the plant. The roots of this flower were once used to treat rattlesnake bites.

Cream of the Crops

California's principal agricultural products:

Every year, California grows more than 300,000 tons (304,800 metric tons) of grapes, and...Wine is made from grapes. California produces 17 million gallons (64,345,000 liters) of wine every year, and...Raisins are dried grapes. Fresno is called the "Raisin Capital of the World."

Chickens

Beef Cattle

Grapes

Oranges

Peanuts

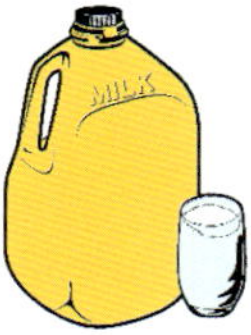
Milk

Seafood

Tomatoes

Corn

Turkeys

Wheat

More turkeys are raised in California than in any other state in the U.S.

First/Big/Small/Etc.

At 300 feet (91 meters), the giant sequoia located in California's Kings Canyon National Park was named the national Christmas tree.

California's smallest national historic site is the Eugene O'Neill National Historic Site in Danville.

The first Pueblo in Los Angeles was started in 1781.

Earl Gilmore's horse-drawn tank-type vehicle was said to be the world's first gas station in 1909.

Castroville's first "Artichoke Queen" in 1947 was a young woman named Norma Jean. She went on to become famous actress Marilyn Monroe.

The Hollywood Bowl is the world's largest outdoor amphitheater.

The "most crooked street in the world" is Lombard Street in San Francisco.

The Central Valley Irrigation Project is the world's largest irrigation system.

In the 1850s, California's first ski races were held at La Porte (Rabbit Creek).

Sequoia National Park contains the world's largest living tree. Its trunk is 102 feet (31 meters) in circumference.

Festivals

Tournament of Roses, New Year's Day—Pasadena

Chinese New Year celebration—San Francisco and Los Angeles

National Orange Show—San Bernadino

Jumping Frog Jubilee—Calaveras County

Fortuna Rodeo—Fortuna

Monterey Jazz Festival—Monterey

California State Fair—Sacramento

Old Spanish Days Fiesta—Santa Barbara

Lone Pine Film Festival—Lone Pine

Hollywood Christmas Parade—Hollywood

Holidays

Important Dates:

New Year's Day, *January 1*

Martin Luther King Jr. Day, *3rd Monday of January*

Presidents' Day, *3rd Monday of February*

California Poppy Day, *April 6*

Cinco de Mayo, *May 5*

Memorial Day, *last Monday in May*

Independence Day, *July 4*

Labor Day, *1st Monday in September*

Admission Day, *September 9*

Columbus Day, *2nd Monday in October*

Veterans Day, *November 11*

Thanksgiving Day, *4th Thursday in November*

Famous Food

California is famous for the following delicious foods!

Quesadillas
Monterey Jack Cheese
Wine
Sourdough bread
Ghirardelli chocolates
Grapes
Chilies
Wonton
Sushi
Sun-dried Tomatoes

Which one is your favorite?

Famous Food

TAKING CARE OF BUSINESS

Petroleum and natural gas generate about 3/4 of California's mining income. Other industries include: the motion picture industry, transportation, equipment, food products, electrical equipment, and machinery.

California is home to many manufacturing plants. Some of them produce: electronic components and equipment; airplanes; food processing; petroleum; computers and computer software.

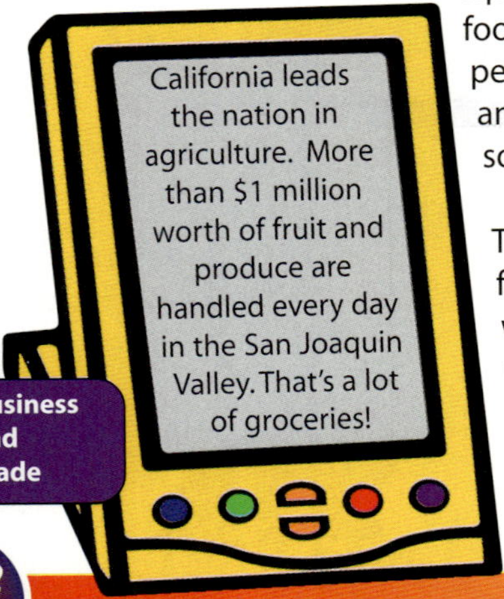

California leads the nation in agriculture. More than $1 million worth of fruit and produce are handled every day in the San Joaquin Valley. That's a lot of groceries!

The Santa Clara Valley, famous for fruit trees, was transformed by the manufacture of silicon chips. Now the area is called Silicon Valley.

oks & W

California Trivia compiled by Lucy Poshek & Roger Naylor
Death Valley's Scotty's Castle; The Story Behind the Scenery by Stanley W. Paher
It Happened in Northern California by Erin H. Turner
It Happened in Southern California by Noelle Sullivan
More Than Petticoats; Remarkable California Women by Erin H. Turner
Quest for the Dutchman's Gold; The 100-year Old Mystery! by Robert Sikorsky
Sequoia–Kings Canyon; The Story Behind the Scenery by William C. Tweed
Tales of Mexican California by Antonio Coronel
The Gold Rush by Bobbie Kalman
The Gold Rush by Liza Ketchum

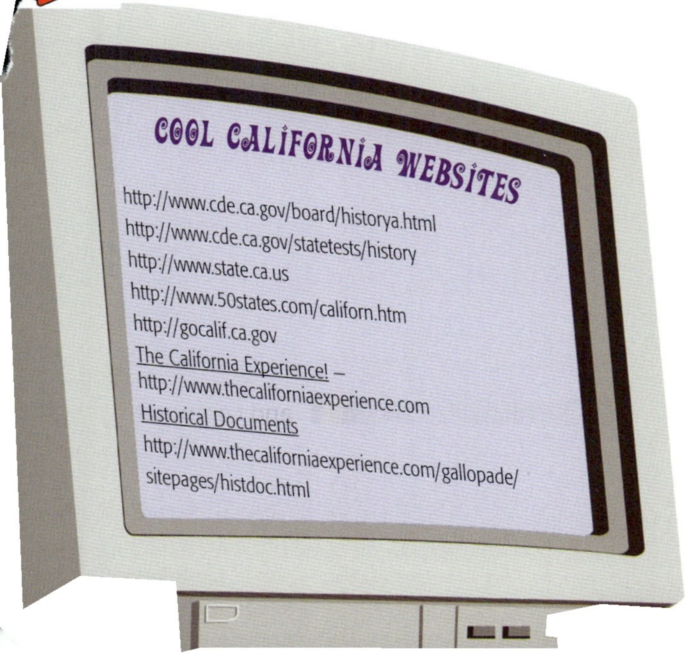

California Glossary

Glossary Words

Gold Rush–sudden flood of people to a place where gold has been discovered

Irrigate–to move the natural flow of water to a dry area to provide water for plants

Mission–Catholic church where native inhabitants were brought to be taught Christianity and to be prepared to become subjects of the Spanish king

Mother Lode–a rich or important veinlike deposit of a mineral such as gold

Pony Express–mail service which operated by relays of pony riders

Presidio–a military post

Pueblo–small farming settlements

Terminus–ending point